Green Jell-O
&
Red Punch:

# The heinous
# <u>Truth!</u>
# about Utah!

...and
Southeast
Idaho

by

C.L. Crosby

Nez-Percé Press

San Francisco

# Green Jello & Red Punch:
# The heinous Truth! about Utah!

by C. L. Crosby and an unnamed white female inmate of Poina the Mou'n.

ISBN 1-930074-05-0
LCCN: 2002100307

Cover design, page design and text icons: Idintdoit Design
Chapter illustrations & Celestial Kingdom by C.L. Crosby
Fonts: Jaft ITC, Avant Garde, Techno
Printing: Poina the Mou'n Inmate Press

Nez-Percé Press
San Francisco, CA  94107
(415) 267-5978

# Table of false witness

# Dedication

for

nancy blosch

# part one:

# why you should not sue us

# INTRODUCTION
## and disclaimer

We really don't mean any of this and it is all made up. We never lived in Utah and have no idea what the state is like. But if we knew, I'm sure we would want to live there and would be nice to our neighbors (assuming they speak to us) and would obey all the laws and not dye our hair any unnatural colors. No references herein are to real people, especially not the guy in prison for child molestation. We just imagined that people might be in prison for child molestation. Maybe in another state. And we are sorry about suggesting that there may be married men in Utah who are gay. Maybe we were thinking of Michael Huffington, and to our knowledge, he never set foot in the state of Utah.

# further legal disclaimer

As we said in our legal disclaimer, above, we really don't mean any of this and it is all made up. We are especially sorry for suggesting any Republicans might be gay. So if we sound like we know what we are talking about, or if we sound like we actually live in Utah, we don't. And we didn't. And actually, you have to admit, this stuff in this book is really too absurd to be real. It is simply not believable. And that is what our lawyer says will keep us from getting sued.

# ACKNOWLEDGMENTS
## and further legal disclaimer

The author and publisher acknowledge the contributions of Utah exiles and deportees across the country who have contributed to this highly imaginary and in-no-way-intended-to-be-considered-true book that is in no way based on their personal experiences and knowledge and should in no way prevent them from moving up in the U.S. State Department, FBI, Disneyland and other organizations heavily populated by Mormons. We also apologize in advance to the Mormon Church® for inaccurately referring to it as the "Mormon Church®" when, just prior to the 2002 winter games whose name we cannot mention or we will be sued, the Mormon Church® changed its name from "The Church of Jesus Christ of Latter-Day Saints (the 'Mormons®')®" to the "Church of Jesus

Christ®." However, the contributors to this book have spent years trying to recover from the pain of having lived in Utah in their imaginations (since nothing in this book is based on fact) and the mention of the "Church of Jesus Christ®" was not sufficient to bring them out of their usual catatonic state where they lie in a fetal position, rock back and forth, and say over and over "Dan, Phil, and Andy, Carpet Experts Open 'Til 6" while chewing on the edge of a Log Cabin quilt tote bag from Mormon Handicraft®. It was only the invocation of the terms "Mormon®" and "Mormon Church®" that brought forth the painful, repressed, inaccurate and imaginary memories of Utah expressed in this book.

Finally it should be noted that many contributors, having grown up in Utah, have been hampered by their lack of exposure to, and resulting inability to distinguish between controlled and illegal substances and their legal counterparts. Hence, they have drunk considerable vodka thinking it was gasoline, smoked parsley thinking it was marijuana, ingested meth tabs thinking they were aspirin, and have even, mistaking them for contact lenses, placed hits of windowpane acid on their eyeballs. This unintentional drug use has impaired their brain capacity considerably. Further, they have been burdened by countless unwanted children based on their inadequate sex education (and the official Church policy denying that nudity exists), causing them to confuse Cool Whip for contraceptive foam, PEZ candy for birth control pills, and penises for one-eyed snakes. Having so many kids (most of whom are now in foster care) has made them quite dumb and lacking in credibility.

# CONTRIBUTORS

Fourteen people fear excommunication from the Mormon Church® for contributing to this book. Contributors to this book who were so ignernt they allowed their real names to be used are:

**E. J. Young**: Former East High School basketball star, now an albino woman playing guitar in a Lesbian band in San Francisco who has named her new breasts "Urim and Thummim" after the two martini glasses that Joseph Smith used to translate the Book of Mormon into English from its original language of crumbs, fish bones and olive pits left on gold-colored plates following a Masonic fundraising dinner in Palmyra, New York.

**Wangarimwnan Rwjnennsnnm**: Excommunicated Tongan gang member now a showgirl of indeterminate race in an Asian transvestite bar in New York.

# FURTHER DISCLAIMER
## and tribute to
## Randy Brigham Young

Finally, it should be noted that any coincidence in the names of any of the purely fictitious people in this book and real people named "Young," is purely due to the randiness of the Church's second president, Brigham Young, who, via 55 relationships that today would be considered adulterous affairs and child molestation, produced more than 56 offspring surnamed Young whose progeny crowd Utah classrooms, juvenile courts, and freeways. These "marriages" were about as serious as those of death row inmates and the prison molls who troll the visiting areas in states that allow conjugal visits: eight of the first eleven marriages were to women who were married to other men and 47 of the 55 wives had other husbands—before, during, or after Brigham Young. Young was constantly being sued for divorce. Three young (under the age of 20) wives divorced him before they ever even lived with him. When he was sued for divorce, he would argue in court that the marriage was not legally valid. In other words, Young was the brilliant creator of the concept of "having it both ways"—instantly married when he wanted sex with a teenager, instantly not married when sued for alimony. For this reason alone he is deserving of all the respect he gets in the patriarchal state of Utah.

# part two:

# Utah-K
# or how ta understand what
# we be sayin

Snowmobile - snowmobill or
        snowsled

# Abbreviations used in Utah speech

| | |
|---|---|
| "f—" | flip |
| "f———n" | flippin |
| "g———n" | gosh darn |
| "d—k" | donk (ey) |
| "s—t" | shoot |
| OMH | Oh-my-heck |

## Pronunciation key

| | |
|---|---|
| appreciate | preshiate |
| to | ta |
| hunting | huh'in |
| hurricane | hurkin |
| cute | cuuuuuuuttttttteeee!!!!!!! |
| Juab (County) | Jew-Ab |
| for | fer |
| conference | conf'rnce (the yearly meeting of the Mormon Church® more successful than the Native American rain dance in ensuring rainfall.) |
| for sure | fer shur |
| trail | trell |
| Sale | Sell |
| Feel | Fill ("I fill terrible") |

17

*— till (True dog's tell is full of bumes.)*

| | |
|---|---|
| my hat | mat |
| ignernt | ignorant |
| county | couny |
| sacrilegious | sacerlijus!! |
| yes | yabetcha, heck-yeah |

## Definitions

*MAV's Mormon Assault Vehicle —*

**MPCs** Mormon Personnel Carriers—the largest possible SUVs, most often Subur-
bans. Used to transport families of 12.

**ward** A large parking lot full of MPCs with a
one-story brick building in the middle
where male Mormons spend the entire day on Sundays. Typically white
brick with lavender marbleized windows. Always topped with a rod. (See
"Hold to the Rod" below). There are
now "southwestern" looking wards
and stake centers and other contemporary architectural details from the
late 1980's. A side note on architectural details in Mormon buildings: Older
Utah homes often have two front

Outfit - Rig

doors. In polygamist homes, each wife had her own parlor and visitin' space though she shared the kitchen and rest of the house. Giving wives their own personal spaces kept them from stabbing each other with kitchen implements.

**stake**  A larger parking lot full of MPCs with a one-story brick building in the middle where male Mormons spend the entire day on Sundays. Typically white brick with lavender marbleized windows. Always topped with a rod. (See "Hold to the Rod" below). Wedding receptions and funeral services are often held at the local stake center. Important to note here: If you stumble into either one of these services it may be hard to tell which one you are attending, given that the tone, mood, clothing and food are the same at weddings and funerals. Look for the mint cups and a champagne fountain filled with water to be sure it is a wedding. (If invited to a Mormon wedding reception please get specific directions and addresses and verify you have the right couple before setting your gift down. You may spend a good hour before realizing it is the wrong wedding. Retrieving the gift from the wrong couple can be awkward.)

**temple** "Where the glue is." Where you get "sealed" to your relatives for all time <u>and</u> eternity. (A plus for some families, a minus for others.)

**time** Time (as in "half-time" at the BYU-Utah game).

**eternity** A really, really long time (as in sitting on wooden benches during two days of Mormon Church® conf'rnce at the Mormon Tabernacle).

**temple mints** Mints with the impression of the Mormon Temple, served at Mormon weddings along with three sugar cookies per person and a cup of red punch.

**excommunication** Being expelled from the Mormon Church for, <u>inter alia</u>, criticizing the Church, following the polygamist teachings of Brigham Young, or showing a nonMormon the way to the nearest liquor store. Many no-longer-faithful spend years attempting to get excommunicated so as to stop the barrage of Church telemarketers attempting to bring the straying back into the flock.

**bishop** The Kinko's® co-worker who is the head of the neighborhood ward.

**prophet** The former Kinko's® co-worker who is the spiritual head of the whole Mormon Church®.

**profit** The money made by the Mormon Church® from tithing and shrewd investments in Coca-Cola® and other Mormon-banned products.

**bear testimony** Standing up in Church and saying disgraceful things about yourself, your friends, and your family. A requirement of the Mormon faith.

**Member** Member of the Mormon Church®.

**Celestial Kingdom®** Decorated in discount store Louis XIV, it is the highest of the three levels of heaven where only the most worthy and "sealed" go to sit on small chairs and think about Babar and Celeste. To get to the Celestial Kingdom, you have to be a married worthy male or married ("sealed") to a married worthy male. (Same-sex sealings do not qualify.) Some believe that the Mormon propensity to obesity has to do with extended thoughts about Babar and Celeste in this lifetime. The few Mormon teens who venture out of state to college and read Milton are usually shocked to learn that the Mormon concept of the heavens and hell, paradise and darkness, are lifted therefrom. (The Mormon Church® attorneys asked that we include this statement: "Wheretofor Milton failed to procure a timely registration of these terms with either the

U.S. Copyright or Trademark Office, henceforth any use of said terms by the Church Formerly Referred to as the Church of Jesus Christ of Latter Day Saints (the 'Mormons'®)® is entirely and wholly lawful and challenge thereof would fail in a court of law in the State of Utah whose judges are wholly and entirely <u>Members</u>.")

**Telestial Kingdom®** Where the less worthy Mormons go to sit on Lay-Z Boy® recliners and watch televised (hence, "<u>tele</u>stial") reruns of BYU-Utah football games.

**Terrestrial Kingdom®** A Rousseau-like jungle kingdom dominated by ATVs (all-terrain vehicles, hence "<u>terre</u>strial") where the unblessed Mormons (those who drank beer while snowmobiling) and nonMormons go to provide warranty services on electronic equipment and to deliver catered Chuck-a-Rama® meals to worthy Mormons via ATVs.

**outer darkness**   Mormon hell.

**general authorities**   Old men.

**council of the 12**   <u>Really</u> old men.

**CTR**   Celestial Tally Registrar. People who keep track of who gets to go to the various levels of heaven based upon their deeds on earth and marital status. These individuals wear a ring with the "CTR" abbreviation indicating their ability to divine this. Oddly enough many young children attending primary church services also wear these as well as closeted gay teenagers (usually on the ring finger after puberty).

**sacrament** Wonder Bread and water served in the same small condiment cups used for mints at weddings and funerals. Bread is torn by a pimply-faced nose-picking 15-year-old "MAN" (manhood = holding the Mormon priesthood, which worthy males of 15 years and older may do).

**free agency** Why the bishop's 14-year-old daughter gets an abortion and yours has to get married. Why the bishop's wife gets to use birth control and yours doesn't.

**funny underwear** See garments.

**garments** Funny, protective underwear worn by people sealed in the temple. Also a way to identify perpetrators, as in "the alleged rapist wore only Temple Garments." They may also protect wearers from skin cancer as wearers are never to expose bare skin in public, even at the swimming pool. Garments contain sacred protective symbols on the nipples and belly button, symbols that look like they were made when the darning feature on grandma's sewing machine ran amuk.

**garment lines** Visible indicia of garments on the upper arm and mid-thigh that get you free drinks in some bars in San Francisco and other cities of the Devil.

**"hold to the rod®"** Mormon Church® slogan favored by gay Mormons. Suspected of having to do with their training on their missions. (Missionaries "hold to the rod®.")

**missionary reunions** A gathering where missionaries are introduced into a putatively heterosexual society after two years during which every waking and sleeping second is spent with a same-sex companion.

**Mormon polygamists** Randy old guys who invented a religious justification for having sex with teenage relatives. Monuments can be seen throughout the state in honor of their wily ingenuity.

**place or "the place"** Salt Lake Valley. The term Brigham Young poetically used to describe the holy valley that ended the pioneers' long journey to the ~~salty wasteland~~ promised land. The entire utterance, which school children carefully and painstakingly memorize is "This is the Place®." Coincidentally, it is also the official greeting at the Utah State Prison, aka Poina the Mou'n.

**revelation** Vision from God to the prophet to bring Church policy into compliance with federal laws or to avoid loss of funding or to increase financial gain. Examples: A 1970's revelation that African-American men were worthy of serving as Mormon priests that coincidentally coincided with the enactment of federal civil rights laws; relaxed alcoholic beverage laws for the MOlympics; BYU's sudden rise as leading college basketball and football teams; a revelation that Coca-Cola® is okay for Church members to drink following the Church's investment in bottling plants.

**sister-wives** Buck-toothed 13-year-old girls who are kept stupid so they will have sex with their smelly, lecherous uncles.

**tithing** The 10% of your income you pay to the Church each month in lieu of paying for health insurance for your family of 14. "10% and you're in."

**church** Presumed in all cases, upper case and lower, to be the Mormon Church®. As in "Are you a church member?" or simply "Are you a <u>member</u>?"

**MOlympics** The 2002 winter games whose name we cannot mention or we will be sued, procured at an irresponsible cost to taxpayers to benefit wealthy <u>Members</u>, to showcase the Mormon Church® and to give the misimpression that Utah is a place where you can get a drink, party into the night, and live in harmony with people of other races, cultures, and faiths.

# part three:

# Beehive state basics

# beehive state basics

Do NOT believe the rumors, we DO sell alcohol in Utah. But do NOT try to find retail outlets by looking under Beer, Wine, or Alcohol in the Yellow Pages. All alcohol is sold by the State in infinitesimal outlet stores hidden from sight of the general populace and unmarked by large signs or billboards. Do not TRY to find one by asking your Utah Volunteer Guide. If they speak your language, they are a returned missionary and do not know where the liquor stores are or will not admit it in public. You will easily find an alcoholic drink on your return flight. However, you will not find mini bottles of liquor here even with the newly relaxed temporary laws put in place for the "MOlympics®," also known as "the 2002 winter games whose name we cannot mention or we will be sued."

Don't laugh at the names (LaVar, LaMont, DelVora, Lehi, Moroni, Aldean, Brigham, or Etta-Mae, etc.). All names are divined and beyond gentile humor.

Don't offer your Utah Volunteer Guide a cup of coffee or tea, regardless of how cold it is or how miserable they look. It is against their religion. Instead offer them cold drinks, such as Coca-Cola® or Mountain Dew®.

That green stuff is not mold. It is Jell-O®, the official State dessert. You might try to taste ALL the 3,456,237 recipes for green Jell-O® salad during your visit. The amazing versatility of Jell-O® is celebrated daily across this pretty great state. Add raisins, carrots or canned fruit cocktail and you have a salad for any occasion.

The Relief Society is NOT a group of citizens who clean public restrooms. They are groups of mothers who specialize in quilts, casseroles and green Jell-O® salad. They meet weekly to exchange quilt patterns, casserole recipes, and interesting variations of green Jell-O® salad. In fact, they are SO dedicated, they dress like quilts, their hair is done to look like their favorite casserole, and they jiggle just like Jell-O®. (Speaking of public restrooms, public sex in Utah is still a viable option and the restrooms at the Church office building have proven ideal for this.)

Don't get lost in downtown Salt Lake. You can go north or south on West Temple, or east or west on North Temple or South Temple, but you can't go north on Main Street anymore. The BIG mountains, and all alpine events are on the East side. A large pond and little mountains are to the west. If you're driving and it starts to smell really bad, you're too far west.

That middle finger wave from so many of the residents is their way of signaling their intent to change lanes, cut over four lanes, or beat you to the off-ramp. They may also wave this way to welcome you into an open parking space.

Remember that concealed weapons are legal in Utah, especially when thinking of re-turning the middle finger wave to any of our friendly Utah drivers.

We don't use profanity in Utah. We use only elder-approved expressions (gosh, gul-durn, dad-gumit, golly, jeminy, frick, frick off, frick up, get fricked, and that frickin shoot).

Our bible is better than your bible, our prophet is better than yours (ours is still alive), our history is more true than yours, and nobody is allowed to laugh about the Church except [political cartoonist] Pat Bagley or ["Mormon peacemaker" columnist] Robert Kirby.

We don't wear "Funny Underwear," "Jesus Jumpers," "Holy Rompers," or "Rocky Mountain Surfing Suits!" We wear blessed undies and it's considered bad taste to ask to see them and NO they are not available as souvenirs.

If a Utahn introduces you to his six wives, please do not say something STUPID like "Isn't that illegal?" Remember again, the concealed weapon law.

We don't do pornography either. That includes the XXX stuff, the X stuff, the hard-R stuff, the PG stuff with bad language or body parts below the neck and above the knee, and anything you can find at Cahoots (878 E. 900 So.), Blue Boutique (2106 So. 1100 E.), Mischievous (559 So. 300 W.), Dr. John's (6885 So. State), and other sinful establishments. We don't do Internet porn, phone porn, video porn, magazine porn, book porn, or Biology Class porn. However, if you are a member of the International Olympic Organizing Committee®, please let your Utah Volunteer Guide know, so a friendly Escort can be provided with your complementary scholarship to a Utah school.

You won't find any businesses open or community activities here on Sundays all-day, Monday evenings, Tuesday afternoons,

Wednesday evenings, Friday afternoons, or Saturday mornings. These are all regularly scheduled Church times and you will be expected to eat, dance, party, and recreate around them.

Finally, we really welcome you, your religion, and your diversity here, so PLEASE enjoy your stay!

# Gettin to know who we is

If you are from Utah. . . .

1. You've never met any celebrities, not even the Osmonds.

2. Your idea of a traffic jam is ten cars waiting to pass a tractor on the highway.

3. "Vacation" means going to Wendover, NV.

4. You've seen all the biggest bands ten years after they were popular.

5. You measure distance in minutes.

6. You know several people who have hit a deer.

7. Your school classes were canceled because of cold.

8. Your school classes were canceled because of heat.

9. You've ridden the school bus for an hour each way.

10. You've had to switch from "heat" to "A/C" in the same day.

11. You think ethanol makes your truck "run a lot better."

12. Stores don't have bags; they have sacks.

13. You see people wearing bib overalls at funerals and weddings.

14. You see a car running in the parking lot at the store with no one in it except a three-year-old child with no car seat no matter what time of the year it is.

15. You end your sentences with an unnecessary preposition. Example: "Where's my coat at?" or "If you go to town I wanna go with."

16. All the festivals across the state are named after a fruit, vegetable, grain, or animal.

17. You install security lights on your house and garage and leave both unlocked.

18. You think of the major four food groups as beef, pork, soda pop, and Jell-O® salad with carrots.

19. You only own 3 spices: salt, pepper, and ketchup.

20. Driving is better in the winter because the potholes are filled with snow.

21. You think everyone from a different state has an accent.

22. You think sexy lingerie is tube socks and a flannel nightie.

23. You think that deer season is a national holiday.

24. You know which leaves make good toilet paper.

25. You know all four seasons: Almost Winter, Winter, Hotter than Hell, and Construction.

26. You happily pay a quarter more for fry sauce (a secret sauce comprised of equal parts ketchup and mayonnaise to dip your french fries in).

27. You actually understand all of these jokes and forward them to your friends.

Note: The foregoing was from a forwarded e-mail from employees of the State tourism office who are afraid of losing their jobs and/or their volunteer positions at the winter games whose name we cannot mention or we will be sued.

Mormon Heaven

# part four:

# Guide to Utah geography

# Ya know yer in <u>Utah</u> when:

You begin to think smoking might be a right worth protecting.

The air feels sticky from hair spray.

Adults say, "Let's go get shitfaced."

You feel like shooting heroin just to prove a point, though you can't recall what the point is.

You feel guilty about having a beer.

You can breathe second hand smoke in a bar, unlike in California.

You are nervous about going into a liquor store.

You can never remember the rules for ordering a drink.

You stop at a stop sign and forget to go.

Parents of people killed by cops say, "Well, he deserved it."

Relatives of murdered people say, "We're happy we'll be in heaven together."

A drive-by shooting is when someone shoots at a car as it drives by their front yard.

Scrapbooking is considered an extreme sport for women.

Ordering a cup of coffee is a political statement.

"The Y" doesn't mean the YMCA, but Brigham Young University.

Funerals are happy occasions.

The most stylishly dressed people are wearing Polarfleece.

People wearing all black look out of place.

The most left-wing liberals are anti-choice and pro-gun.

The only pro-choice, anti-gun party is the 3-member Socialist Workers' Party.

You don't know anyone who has used public transportation.

Most women thought they'd never have a job outside the home; most women have a job outside the home.

Parents often leave their kids at rest stops.

All the vehicles on the road, including limos, are actually pickup trucks.

People ask you what ward you are in, if you're married, where you went on your mission, and how many kids you have within the first 30 seconds of meeting you.

You are asked in job interviews if you are "a Member."

Coffee is considered a gateway drug.

Wearing seatbelts is controversial.

You can buy a bolt of fabric or a gun in a mall.

Blind people can get hunting permits.

Nearly everyone is big, white, and has a concealed weapon permit.

Adults dress like toddlers (e.g., pastel teddy bear sweats and gingham holsters).

Jell-O® is served as a main course.

Gravemarkers read "Mother. Mother. Mother. Mother. Father," or "Father. Wife. Other wives."

The cops have shut down a meth lab in your neighborhood.

Every woman you meet is on antidepressants.

Adults drink red and green punch.

Half of the kids in the kindergarten class have the last name "Young." The other half are named Smith.

Every kid you meet is on Ritalin.

The grocery stores have ONLY supersized items.

When you ask what kind of wine a restaurant has the answer is "red, white, or pink."

Pacific Islanders are called "Polynesians," Asians are called "Orientals," and Latinos are called "Spanish."

Anyone who is not blonde is considered to
fall into one of the above categories.

The bride and the mother of the bride are
both pregnant.

Everyone who is not Mormon, including
Jews, are called "gentiles."

People are considered to have "sexual
preferences" that they can change
on whim.

Interracial marriages are frowned upon
because the color of your skin helps deter-
mine the level of heaven you go to and
we should all marry someone who will be
on our same level.

High school girls have already picked out the names for their seven kids by the time they graduate.

Women who don't move during sex can truthfully tell their bishops they are not "sexually active."

People take their TVs when they go camping.

Every child is "an accident" and "the last one."

The public school district provides high school girls mini hope chests and samples of silver patterns.

One of the two largest health insurers in the state (IHC) won't insure Utahns who "travel out of Utah more than once or twice a year."

A 16-1 ratio of children to caregiver in a home day care center is considered good.

The state pays a "Porn Tzar" to look at porn but she is not authorized to do anything about it.

Girls have their entire weddings planned by the time they are 15.

Ten-year-old girls wear lipstick.
And pantyhose.

Teenagers get really nervous when you order coffee from them at a coffee shop.

The only publicity for high school reunions is a sign in front of the school; children are invited and alcohol is not.

It is considered okay for Mormons to drink alcohol during huntin' season, over the State line ("over ta Wendover fer some prime rib") or any time they are in a Recreational Vehicle.

You're 45 and still figuring out how to smuggle alcohol.

This list hasn't changed since 1977.

# Ya know yer In <u>Salt Lake City</u> when:

Pedestrians actually wait for the light to turn green.

All roads lead to Temple Square.

You recognize the value of owning a gun after seeing your 50th bronze statue of a happy pioneer family downtown.

Everyone downtown is carrying a small floral suitcase containing their temple underwear and concealed weapon.

The newspaper does not advertise R-rated movies.

Democrats have given up on voting.

# Ya know yer in <u>West Valley City</u> when:

The women are still wearing hair-sprayed claw bangs, shoulder pads and stirrup pants in day glow colors.

Your wedding is in your gang colors.

Your manicure consists of more than three colors (at least one metallic) and a gold angel charm.

Your car cost more than your education.

You drive a t-top Trans Am and think you have succeeded in life.

The only college you've heard of is the beauty college.

You hope to keep your teeth through your 40's.

No one has heard of voting.

People with dice hanging from their rear view mirrors don't know the word "camp."

Your hair stylist has a mullet.

Everyone has been shot at least once by a blood relative.

People do their own tatoos.

Marrying up is marrying someone with a
possibility of parole.

Your Easter best is white high heeled
pumps with jeans.

You have "registered at Mervyn's" printed
on your wedding invitations.

You consider your nails your best asset and
those who know you agree.

There are low-riders in your wedding party.

Vintage 70's clothes are considered contemporary.

You feed your baby from a bottle because you heard nursing can diminish your breast size in the long run.

None of the moms know how they got pregnant.

All parentage has been confirmed by DNA.

Your new boyfriend has gotten both you and your mother pregnant.

# Ya know yer in <u>Park City</u> when:

You think you're in Colorado but you haven't crossed a state line.

No one is from Utah.

Everyone came to Utah to ski for a year.

People actually know the word nightlife.

Everyone is tan and in real estate.

Democrats vote.

People are just like those in other parts of
the country except they drink more.

People have their jeans dry-cleaned.

Harry Reams is a realtor and not a porn star
(not anymore anyway).

By age 50, most everyone has had too
much sun and too much to drink.

Every resident had sex with every other
resident at least once in the '70s, whether
they remember it or not.

# Ya know yer at the Sundance Film Festival when:

People ride in limos even though the town
is only a block long.

The town is filled with New Yorkers trying to
look like Utahns and with Utahns trying to
look like New Yorkers.

No one is not talking on a cell phone.

Prices are twice those of ski season,
quadruple those of summer.

You swear every guy you see is Ethan Hawke and every woman is Uma Thurman.

For ten days locals say "film" instead of "movie."

# Ya know yer in <u>Utah County</u> when:

Video stores edit sex scenes out of movies they rent.

Folks deny anyone drinks but Alanon meetings are abundant.

The high level of creativity in the county is reflected in the slogan for the mall: "Where the stores are."

You can get a Ph.D. in Art History from BYU without being aware that any artists ever depicted nudes.

You have medium dark hair and you are thought of as exotic.

The Bridal Fair is held at the high school.

Every surface is covered with a blue and white banner with a "Y" on it.

Every conversation begins with "Did you go to BYU?"

There are no pregnant unmarried teenagers. They are all married.

Catholics have to avoid American Fork for fear of being stoned to death.

Coffee houses in Lindon are referred to as taverns.

You carry an extra set of clothes in your Camper. One for when you visit coffee shops/taverns and one set to go home in.

You mother is called a whore by your class-mate because she allows you to decide for yourself about going to the Mormon Church®.

Your next door neighbor is a whore who your classmate's father visits late at night.

# Ya know yer in <u>Moab</u> when:

You can order a warm chevre and arugula salad and they know what you are talking about.

No one is from Utah.

Everyone came here to mountain bike for a year.

When people hear the word "steak" they think of meat and not the Mormon stake center.

There are people who are over 30 and not married.

Democrats vote.

You have to go to Hell to cool off in the summer.

People know how to read maps.

70% of the men are wearing tight black bike shorts.

None of the men wearing tight black bike shorts are worrying that wearing tight black bike shorts will make them gay.

100% of the men driving their RVs past the men in tight black bike shorts (on their way to shoot up some rock art) are worrying that looking at men in tight black bike shorts will make them gay.

# Ya know yer in <u>Rural Utah</u> when:

Every house is a trailer or is designed to look like a trailer.

Shooting up petroglyphs is the most popular sport.

By law, every home must have a gun.

Antique stores need the subtitle "Old Stuff."

Your bartender has a trilobite tattoo.

The only restaurant in town is in a retrofitted truck-trailer.

By law, all recreation must be loud and motorized.

The town believes its designation of itself as a "United Nations-free zone" has indeed prevented the U.N. from establishing a presence there.

You see a man's wives traveling in sets and two paces behind him.

The cops have busted three meth labs on your block.

The county's ethnic rivalry is based on whether you are a GM truck guy, a Chevy guy, or a Ford guy.

Officials say "Why do we need the U.S. Constitution when we have the Utah Constitution?"

A bumper sticker reads: "I'd be gone if I could find a paved road out of here."

Public safety announcements for the county are made in the ward on Sunday.

When the sheep start being more attractive then the local girls (you thank God you're gay and you have a steady camping buddy).

You enter a medieval feudal system where the family owning the biggest doublewide thinks they are the Monarchs and everyone else is beneath them.

If you get a divorce your ex-wife is still your cousin.

People wave when they pass you
on the highway.

You can lose your standing in the
community if your in-laws find beer cans in
your garbage or if you have any relatives
who drink alcohol. (On the other hand if
nobody knows you are a drunk you still
remain a saint.)

You are followed in stores because your
suspicious behavior is having dark hair
and dark eyes.

You aren't prejudice against the Native
Americans, you just wish they would move
off the reservation so your property values
could go up, after all it was God who
turned their skin brown as a reminder of
their sins.

# Ya know yer in <u>Carbon County</u> when:

People brag that their mine's killed more miners than any other mine in the county.

The town brothel is still in use.

People invite you to dinner in their Tuff Shed.

"The Church" means the Catholic Church.

## Ya know yer are in <u>a casino in</u> <u>Wendover, Nevada</u> when:

You see your bishop drinking a Lite beer.

You see your 18-year-old daughter has finally gotten a job.

If you have dark hair and eyes you are told to get back to work.

# part five:

## Tips ta help ya enjoy yer stay and ta keep ya ouda Poina the Mou'n

# Tips ta keep ya ouda Poina the Mou'n

In Utah, the cop is ALWAYS right.

Anything green can be considered a "salad," including lime Jell-O®, pistacio ice cream, shredded dollar bills, and marijuana. Thus, if you get caught with marijuana you're far better off saying you thought it was a salad than saying you use it to ease the pain of your terminal cancer.

A "covered dish" is a homemade casserole, not a pot with a lid.

It is illegal in Utah to include an unsweetened food on a buffet table.

Utahns DO NOT believe in motorcycle helmets, seatbelts or gun locks. Protect yourself accordingly.

The bronze statues of happy pioneer families all over downtown are actually anti-aircraft detectors equipped with high-powered radar guns installed especially for those winter games whose name we cannot say or we will be sued. Please do not shoot their heads off no matter how annoying they are!

If you are the architect for the prison and you molest Boy Scouts, make sure your design includes an escape tunnel.

If you are looking to marry your cousin, wait until you are 50, then Utah law allows it.

Do NOT ask Mormons why they can drink highly caffeinated Mountain Dew and hot chocolate but not coffee or tea. They don't know!

Do NOT try to start a Gay-Straight Alliance club in a high school in Utah unless you want to become famous and be in a documentary movie shown on PBS. The Salt Lake City School Board banned ALL clubs rather than accept a Gay-Straight club at East High School. It became a source of national ~~embarrassment~~ pride.

Do not confuse LDS (the Church of Jesus Christ of Latter Days Saints) with LSD—with LSD, the illusion eventually wears off.

Kearns is not a social disease and therefore, visiting a brothel in Kearns is not as bad as it sounds, especially if you don't get caught. Magna, however, is a whole 'nuther story.

# part six:

# the heinous TRUTH!
# about Utah!

# The heinous Truth! about Utah!

The 46-ounce insulated soft drink mugs everyone carries with them at all times actually contain Holy Scriptures so that if the person is suddenly facing death, the proper words can be recited by any boy over the age of 8 who has been a Boy Scout.

A newspaper article reported the alleged sexual assault of two preteen girls by the father of a girl who had invited them for a sleepover in a backyard tent. The article said the perpetrator wore only LDS garments.

A state employee in charge of pornography was arrested for soliciting a prostitute on State Street for oral sex. He said looking at the pornography made him do it.

A condominium board in Salt Lake City announced to its residents that "illegal conjugation will not be tolerated." Out of fear, residents quit using the present subjunctive.

A Utah man embezzled money from his mother to pay for his girlfriend's breast implants.

You can let your kids ride in the bed of a pickup truck unrestrained in Utah but not your dogs.

A Utah gynecologist reserves Saturdays to perform abortions on the daughters and granddaughters of wealthy Mormons who arrive at the office disguised in big hats and sunglasses (see "free agency," in the definitions section).

A Salt Lake doctor says approximately half of her female patients have breast implants. Half of her male patients have natural "D" breasts.

A Utah County Commissioner tried to get out of a DUI (driving under the influence of alcohol) by saying he'd picked up a hitchhiker who had offered him a drink of what he thought was coffee but turned out to be vodka. He drank it (apparently unable to differentiate between coffee and vodka because of an inadequate education as a Mormon teenager). Later he changed his story (perhaps because he realized he shouldn't be drinkin' coffee) and said he thought what he was drinkin' was gasoline. (His lawyer asked us to include this statement: "Drinkin' gasoline IS IN NO WHERES prohibited by the Mormon scriptures OR by Utah State law.")

Utah has the highest consumption of hairspray, chewing gum, and ice cream in the nation, and hence the highest rate of teenage pregnancy.

A Utah man left his 2-year-old son in his unheated pickup truck in the middle of winter while he went hunting. The boy, dressed only in his pajamas, got out of the truck to look for his dad and eventually froze to death. The dad was sentenced to 30 days in jail. Rather than carry out this unjust and onerous sentence he shot and killed himself. (His relatives later sued the rescuers for not having found the baby before he froze to death.)

A store that used to have the slogan "Never on Sundays," to curry favor with its Mormon customers is now open on Sundays.

In the 1980's, a Utah County school district prohibited the use of the words "condom," "intercourse," or "penis" in the teaching of sex education. The words "rubber," "bang" and "one-eyed snake" were substituted.

The news reporter who broke the story of the "alleged" bribery to get the winter games whose name we cannot mention or we will be sued said that Utahns are "not the most moral people, but maybe the most self-righteous."

In the late 1980's, Utah adopted the slogan, "Utah, a pretty, great state." The comma was often left out, better reflecting the general consensus of those who live here.

High school graduation requirements in Salt Lake City:

|  | Public | Catholic |
|---|---|---|
| English | 4 years | 4 years |
| Art | 1.5 | 1 |
| Social Studies | 3 | 4 |
| Vocational Ed | 1 | 0 |
| Math | 2 | 3 |
| Science | 2 | 3 |
| Physical Ed. | 1.5 | 1.5 |
| Health | .5 | .5 |
| Electives | 8.5 units | 3.25 units |
| Religion | 0 | 4 |
| Foreign lang. | 0 | 2 |
| Computers | 0 | .75 |
| Total | 24 units | 27 units |

Admission requirements for UC-Berkeley and other prestigious out-of-state universities require a minimum of 2 years of a foreign language (3 recommended) and 3 years of math (4 recommended).

Elementary schools on Salt Lake's West Side are 70%-80% minority (primarily Latino, Southeast Asian and Pacific Islander). Salt Lake is overall 20% Latino. The State Legislature is made up of 99% white (non-Latino) men.

A young female law school graduate was given this job offer by a Salt Lake City law firm: "Our firm is all married, Mormon men. We need someone to go out drinking with clients."

Other interview questions actually asked women in Salt Lake City: "Are you married? Do you plan to get married? If so, how many children do you plan to have?" "What is your maiden name?" "Do you <u>have</u> to work?"

A handwriting assignment in a Salt Lake City middle school required students to copy off the board multiple times, "Baby Jesus was born in a manger." A Jewish girl's objections were "accommodated" by having her sit alone in the hall.

Women in Utah do not allow pregnancy, an everyday occurrence, to interfere with their daily lives. In 2001, a Utah woman injected herself in the stomach with heroin, forgetting that she was eight months pregnant.

Brigham Young University removed Rodin's "The Kiss" and "John the Baptist" sculptures from its Rodin exhibit because they depicted nudity. The Church's official policy is to deny that nudity exists.

Thanks to BYU'S policy of not allowing teachers to show students R-rated movies or clips from them, you can get a degree in film history from BYU without ever having seen an R-rated movie

In the late 1990's the Salt Lake City Council sold a central block of Main Street to the Mormon Church®, which closed it to traffic and free speech. The City turned down similar requests from the Hari Krishnas and Scientologists to purchase portions of Main Street.

A lawsuit was filed in 2001 against a restaurant that gave "missionary discounts." A number of local retailers give discounts to missionaries and/or to Mormons who "moon" to show they are wearing Mormon undergarments.

The Fourth of July is a normal business day in Utah; the big summer holiday with parades and fireworks is the 24th of July, marking the date when the Mormon Pioneers entered the valley in 1847.

A bar in San Francisco, the Hotel Utah, hosts a Mormon Pioneer Day party every 24th of July. The cover charge is waived for people wearing garments and Mormons get free drinks (the favored Mormon beverage, gasoline on the rocks with a twist).

The State authorized the creation of Lake Powell, the Southern Utah boat mecca, even though doing so destroyed considerable ancient Anasazi rock art.

Actual college counseling for girls at Salt Lake City public high schools: "Why would you want to go to a good college and take up a space a boy could have?" "Why would you want to go to college when you're only going to drop out and get married after your sophomore year?" "Why do you want to go out of state? 99% of our students stay in state?" "Why would you want to go to college—don't you want to have a family?"

Academic counseling for girls at a Salt Lake public high school: "Why would you want to take Calculus? Just tell me, <u>when</u> in your life will you <u>ever</u> use Calculus?"

Utah still has polygamists living on welfare in scary run-down rural dwellings with dirty feral cats and dirty feral children running around and playing on discarded toilets and truck transmissions.

Polygamist girls are forced into marriage to much older men (sometimes uncles) at as young as age 13 and lose a chance to get their teeth fixed and play on soccer teams and study abroad during college. Or even go to college at all. Or sometimes even go to high school at all. They are forced to wear heinous burqa-like gingham granny gowns over jeans and clunky hiking boots or tennis shoes (they are <u>not</u> allowed to play tennis).

Take a look at the polygamist men—there's a reason they have to resort to forced marriages.

It is said that a Mormon Church® representative sits in the gallery of the legislature and signals to legislators how the Church wants them to vote by the way he crosses his legs. 80% of Utah men say that they fear crossing their legs at the thigh will signal that they are gay.

Despite a perception that Utahns are healthy, health insurance costs for individual policies in Utah are higher than in California and provide fewer benefits.

A Salt Lake City billboard company refused to post a billboard for a beer named after a famous Mormon polygamist called "Porter

Rockwell Ale." The ad read "Why have just one?"

Brighton ski resort advertises a new lift that seats four skiers: "Wife. Wife. Wife. Husband." It also advertises youth passes with the slogan "Bring 'em Young," a reference to not only Mormon Church® founder polygamist Brigham Young, but to polygamists' tastes for 13-year-olds.

Utah is internationally famous for its 1915 execution of Joe Hill, a songwriter for the IWW (International Workers of the World, the Wobblies). Hill is considered one of the greatest martyrs of the labor movement.

Do NOT try to argue that the Second Amendment's reference to a "well-armed militia" refers to a government militia and not a citizen's right to form a private army. Not even Utah Democrats will argue this. At the

Million Mom March in 2000, NO politician would speak against the alleged right to bear arms.

In November 2001, the Mormon Church® sent humanitarian supplies to Afghanistan including clothing and blankets emblazoned with the Church's name and logo, perhaps unaware that wearing clothing touting Jesus Christ could get an Afghan killed.

Church members consider themselves living "saints," hence, the "Church of Jesus Christ of Latter-Day Saints."

The only things you cannot buy on Sunday in Utah, BY LAW, are liquor and cars. Cars BY LAW cannot be sold on Sundays. This could be because one of the state's biggest car dealers, who also owns the Utah Jazz NBA basketball team, is Mormon. (It seems Sunday, the day you can't buy booze, would be a good day to sell cars.)

The big liquor store on North Temple, which all travelers to the MOlympics will see, was built just before the MOlympics in an attempt to convince visitors that liquor stores are open and obvious, advertised and easy to get to in Utah. This is NOT the case! They are normally hidden away in the basement parking garages of grocery stores and you have to walk through mud and potholes to get to them. They provide shoppers with child-sized shopping carts to humiliate them into feeling they are lushes if they buy enough wine for a dinner party for six.

The Mormon-owed TV station, Channel 5, will be broadcasting commercials for hard liquor during the 17 days of the MOlympics ONLY, again in an attempt to make Utah seem to visitors like a normal place and not an outpost of the Taliban.

In the 1980's a Church Member, Mark Hoffman, blew up a number of other Members he thought would reveal his scheme selling forged Church documents as authentic (including a document purportedly written by a slimy white salamander). This was one of the few times Utah has made it into the national news; other times include the execution of Joe Hill, the execution of Gary Gilmore, and the execution of Ted Bundy (a former University of Utah Law School student executed in Florida). Oh, and the "alleged" bribery involving the 2002 winter games whose name we cannot mention or we will get sued—games designed to polish up Utah's image as a world-class place and not one dominated by religious oddballs and capital felons.

In the 1970's the Prophet warned Mormon women about the dangers of allowing men to view their bare elbows.

In 2001, a Utah attorney defending a boy who killed a 13-year-old pedestrian while drag-racing used the "boys will be boys" defense, claiming that all boys, even the judge, drag race as teenagers. A citizen responded in a letter to the editor suggesting if this assumption is true, perhaps the legal age for driving for boys should be 21.

It is illegal in Utah to: <u>Not</u> drink milk, fish from horseback, detonate a nuclear weapon (though you can possess one), hunt whales, and have sex in an ambulance if it is responding to an emergency call.

In 2002, Utahns were outraged when it was announced they would not be able to carry their concealed nuclear weapons into MOlympic events.

In 2002, the State Legislature passed a law allowing students to carry concealed weapons (including nuclear weapons) into their classrooms in order to protect their right to free speech.

# part seven:

# Gettin along in Utah, a how ta guide

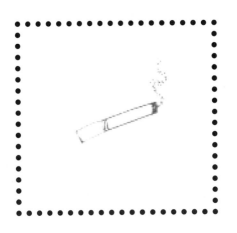

# How ta: Dress in Drag in Utah

Utah law requires cross-dressers to wear a minimum of three items of apparel belonging to their own sex. The following official Utah Drag Queen Matrix was enacted by the legislature in 1992 to assist in complying with State law. (Wearing one item from each column ensures compliance with the law.)

| Item 1 | Item 2 | Item 3 |
| --- | --- | --- |
| tighty-whiteys | condom | fedora |
| Brylcream | waders | boxers |
| jockstrap | cufflinks | fob |
| brogues | suspenders | rifle |
| necktie | pince-nez | condom |
| condom | Old Spice | necktie |
| scout merit badge sash | tool belt | pocket protector |

# How ta:
# Talk Like a Utahn

## Pronouns

Substitute object pronouns for subject pronouns.

"Him and me's goin fishin while the wife rebuilds the transmission."

"Me 'n' her's gettin married in the temple soon as her gets outta jail."

## Verbs

(Study this carefully because Illegal conjugation is considered a sex crime and can get you time out at Poina the Mou'n.)

"They be up ta Cedar fer confer'nce."
Trans: "They are in Cedar City for Mormon Church® conference."

"Them's huh'in over'n East Carbon."
Trans: "They are hunting in East Carbon."

"Him and she, they be goin ta Hurkin."

Trans: "He and she are going to Hurricane [, Utah]."

## Adjectives

Use only Mormon Church Approved Adjectives®—

| | |
|---|---|
| fun | "What a fun dickey!" |
| cute | "Well, fer cute!" |
| special | "That's s'special!" |
| darling | "She's such a darling girl!" |
| ta die fer | "Them espadrilles are ta die fer!" |

Memorize the following cursing matrix (use one term from each column):

| | | |
|---|---|---|
| gosh | dern | sacerlijis |
| dag | golly | heathen |
| friggin | durn | fricked |
| dog | dang | gumit |
| dern | frick | shoot |
| gol | jeminy | friggin |
| flippin | dang | heck |

# How ta:
# Talk Like a Utah Child

"What are you?"

"Our church is the only true church!"

"Ha, ha, ha, yer not goin ta heaven!!"

"That's sacerlijus!!!"

"My parents say we can't play with you!"

# How ta:
## Keep Your Kids in Utah

Raise your kids in Utah.

Take them on vacations to St. George and
Bear Lake only.

Send them to a Utah public high school
where the ACT exam is given, not the SAT
needed to apply to out-of-state colleges.

Put them in Utah public schools whose
college counselors have never heard of
colleges outside of Utah.

Enforce the "English as the Official Language" law so that your kids are unaware

that there are people in the world who speak other than English.

Send them to Utah public schools  whose graduation requirements will preclude them from attending any reputable out-of-state university.

# How ta:
# Avoid Havin ta Pay to Send Yer Kids ta College

Send them to a Utah public high school so they won't find out about college.

Send them to a Utah public high school where they won't get the courses they need to get into college.

Prevent them from learning about contra-
ception so they will get pregnant
and forget about college.

When your kids ask why you can't afford
things like a refrigerator or a phone, say
"It's against our religion!" rather than let-
ting them know it's because you never
went to college and therefore support your
12 children and stay-at-home wife on a
minimum wage job.

Live in rural Utah where your kids will spend
most of their time sucking on gas-soaked
rags and be too dumb to go to college.

# How ta: Make Sure Ya Getta Raise Yer Grandchildren

Raise your children in Utah.

Send them to public schools where they will not learn about birth control.

Send them to the Mormon Church® where they will learn that nice girls are never prepared for sex with birth control, but if sex "just happens" it's okay.

Pay your last dollars in tithing to the Church so you don't have the money to bail your kids out of jail and you will get to raise their kids.

# How Ta:
# Be Faithful to Yer Wife

Have sex with other males only.

Have sex with children only.

Cop a feel every chance you get.

Take advantage of all the "plain brown
paper wrapper" offers on cable tv.

# How ta:
# Look Like a Utah Single Girl

Wear a "waterbra" or spend your college
money on implants.

Get a fake bake (tanning booth tan).

Wear claw (aka "devil") bangs.

If over 25 years old, wear loose denim
jumpers to hide the weight gain from those
five pregnancies.

# How ta:
## Look Like a Utah Guy

Be white and puffy.

Carry a Maverick Big Gulp cup at all times.

Make sure your belly hides your belt.

# How ta:
## Stay Fit Like a Utahn

Push a cart piled with three cases of
Spaghetti Os, five boxes of
diapers, seven cases of Mountain Dew and
20 cartons of cigarettes through Costco.

# How ta:
# Eat Like a Utahn

Do not eat anything that has not been preceded by at least 15 minutes of standing in line or idling in your car.

Eat only from: all-you-can-eat buffets, drive-thrus, or directly from plastic, foil, or styrofoam packaging.

Mormon rules require your stomach contain, at all times, a one-year food supply (hence the prevalence of all-you-can-eat buffets).

If you stomach hurts it means you need to pray, then continue filling up.

Memorize the following Official Utah Jell-O Matrix:

**JELL-O FLAVORS**

**ADDED INGREDIENTS**

| | **Lemon** | **Lime** | **Strawberry** | **Raspberry** | **Orange** |
|---|---|---|---|---|---|
| **carrots & celery** | picnic with the inlaws | Relief Society brunch; teen grounding | summer wedding buffet | Thanks-giving; hospital siege | any buffet or angelic visitation |
| **cottage cheese** | funeral or missionary reunion | anytime, anywhere | Swiss Days; Valentine dance | Christmas Eve dinner | revelation or Halloween party (add black jelly beans) |
| **mini marsh-mallows** | grand-parents' birthday (add prunes) | Polynesian baby blessing | Fourth of July picnic | Pioneer Day picnic | temple dedication; mall opening |
| **pineapple; coconut; banana** | senior citizen luau | Tongan ward dedication | ward banquet; missionary farewell | Christmas brunch; Marion stand-off | Samoan ward dedication |
| **fruit cocktail** | dinner on Monday | dinner on Tuesday | dinner on Wednesday | dinner on Thursday | dinner on Friday |

*The Jell-O Matrix*

From No Man Knows My Pastries: The Secret (Not Sacred) Recipes of Sister Enid Christensen, as told to Roger B. Salazar & Michael G. Wightman (Signature Books, Salt Lake City, 1992). Reprinted with permission of publisher.

# How ta: Get Sex in Utah

Become a Boy Scout Troop Master.

Watch R-rated movies so you will be compelled to solicit a prostitute on State Street.

Go on a mission.

Become a camp Counselor in the Teton Council of the BSA

# How ta:
# Have Sex Like a Utah Man

Get involved civically by researching whether the Victoria's Secret catalog meets the local definition of obscenity.

Become a State official investigating pornography so you can get oral sex from a prostitute on State Street and blame it on the job.

# How ta:
## Have Sex Like a Utah Woman

Push a cart piled with three cases of
Spaghetti Os, five boxes of
diapers, seven cases of Mountain Dew and
20 cartons of cigarettes through Costco.

# How ta:
## Avoid Following Homosexual Urges

Get married and have children.

Redirect your energies into being a Boy
Scout Troop Master.

Deny homosexuality exists.

Beat up gay people.

# How ta: Buy Alcohol in Utah

Use a fake I.D. Even adult nonMormons feel compelled to use a fake I.D. for some reason they haven't sorted out since high school.

# How ta: Get Out of a DUI (driving under the influence of alcohol)

Say you just took a swill of gasoline off the pump out at the Sinclair an as fer as ya know there ain't nuthin illegal bout that.

Say you was drinkin whatcha thought were antifreeze but turned out to be bourbon.

Let the officer know yer a bishop.

# How ta:
# Tell if People Are Mormon

Do they have garment lines? (Check for neckline in V-shape, lines at mid-upper arm and mid-thigh. Use your finger if necessary—this is how the bishops check church-goers every Sunday to make sure they are wearing their garments.)

Do they use the word "cute" in at least every other sentence?

Did they offer you a hand-made basket with a gingham lining filled with home-made jams, scones, and methamphetamine?

Do they seem so nice it kinda creeps you out?

# How ta:
# Determine if Yer New Neighbors
# Are Mormon

Fer sher Mormon:

Garments on clothesline.

Fer sher not Mormon:

New York Times delivered to house on
Sundays.

Maybe Mormon:

Beer cans/liquor bottles/cigarette
butts in trash.
Ammonia smell emanating from house
(meth lab).
Modified treadmill in backyard (evidence
of breeding dogs for dog fights).

# How ta:
# Drive Like a Utahn

Steer with your knee, keeping your hands free to hold your Big Gulp mug and to whack your kids.

Blast your horn when you come up upon bicyclists in the bike lane. This will let them know that you see them.

Let your kids ride in the bed of your pickup. This might provide them some "experiential learning" —seeing what it's like to be a smashed carcass on the highway.

Cancel your insurance after you get your car registered.

"Merge" by stopping on the freeway.

Forget seatbelts. (Friend a mine, his Cusin wund'da died 'cept he was wear'n a seatbelt 'n' could'nt get oudda his truck when he crashed it inta the Top Stop.)

# How ta:
# Make Sense of a Doctor's Visit in Utah

If you are a woman, the doctor will assume you are seeking antidepressants. (Utah has the highest Prozac® & Valium® rate in the country.)

If you are a man, the doctor will assume you are seeking antidepressants to cheer up your wife who is suicidal because you are having an affair and she is home with five kids and is pregnant.

Be aware that Mormon male doctors, dentists, accountants and attorneys have a statutory duty (imposed by the 99% Mormon male legislature) to examine the breasts of all female patients/clients to make sure their implants haven't shifted.

If you are a prescription drug addict, the doctor will assume you became addicted at the Mormon Missionary Training Center.

If you are an unmarried woman seeking birth control, expect to get an "icing before the cake" admonition from your gynecologist.

Your doctor may be suspicious if it turns out you've seen another proctologist in the last 30 days. Getting one rectal exam after another is a ploy well known to Utah doctors.

# How ta: Greet Yer New NonMormon Neighbors

"It would have been nice to have known you."

## How ta: Think Like a Utahn

<u>Unmarried Men</u> (i.e., under 21)
"How much drinkin and drugs can I do and still go on a mission?"
"I hope I'm not gay."

<u>Unmarried Women</u> (i.e, under 18)
"How do I get myself pregnant so he'll marry me, while pretending that I don't know nuthin' about sex?"
"Cosmetology school or exotic dancer career? (Note: Check what escorts make.)"
"Boobs done or ass?"
"New Year's resolution: Improve mind by reading <u>Cosmo</u> every month."

### Married men

"How can I brush against that receptionist's breast and make it seem like I'm reaching for a pencil?"

### Married women

"Shall I take an overdose of sleeping pills or slit my wrists with a razor? A razor would make a mess, but I could do it in a bathtub at a motel and leave a $20 for the maid. But if I checked into a motel, the bishop would think I'm a slut..."

### The Elderly

"LaVerne fer shur is gunna be in the Celestial Kingdom with me 'n' LaDonna, but what about LaRae? (Note: Check to see if I got unsealed from Ray before gettin sealed ta Butch.)"

## How ta: Be a Gentile in Utah

Be a Jew. Mormons consider all
nonMormons, regardless of faith, gentiles.

## How ta: Make Yer Vote Count

Move to a different state.

# part eight:
# Field guide to identifying species of Utahns/Utahnas

# The Utah Republican

### Male

Blond. Suit or "causal wear" consisting of khaki pants, polo shirt and navy jacket with zipper in front, elastic at wrists and waist.

### Female

Blonde. Mid-calf denim skirt or jumper, embroidered sweater, heavy orange face makeup.

### Habitat

Found in McMansion in planned community with duck (or cow) motif in kitchen; three-car and one-RV garage. Alternatively found in pubic forums expressing concern that teaching sex education in schools will turn parents gay.

## Characteristics

Drives SUV, including two blocks to the ward.

Has never taken public transportation.

Wife does "tole."

Think it's fine that the Republicans gerrymandered the Democrats in Salt Lake City out of existence.

Call their coffee table a "hot chocolate table."

Pronounce "croissant" "crescent."

Dad was present for the birth of first child, checked in by phone for other ten.

Worried that 24-year-old daughter is not married and rides a Harley.

Have sent 8 kids on missions.

Have a year's supply of Captain Crunch cereal, Tang, and Pringles in the basement ('cause "yer body is a temple").

Hope the Mormon Church® really is the Only True Church.

Prozac® required for constant worry about who will be with them in heaven and whether they will have reserved seats or will have to wait in line.

# The Utah Democrat

## Male

Blond. Cargo pants, fleece vest, Birkenstocks.
Bruises on head from beating it against the
wall.

## Female

Blonde. Cargo pants, fleece vest,
Birkenstocks.
Bruises on head from beating it against the
wall.

## Habitat

Found in bungalow or aging Victorian on Avenues or "Yale/Harvard" area often in kitchen cooking ratatouille surrounded by collection of Fiestaware dishes from '40s.

## Characteristics

Defeated yet duty-burdened.

Drive SUV.

Has never taken public transportation.

Prozac® required for sense of defeat.

Serves on boards of numerous liberal nonprofits out of sense of duty.

Attends public hearings.

Dad cuts the cord at kids' births.

Votes, despite knowledge that vote doesn't count.

Sends kids to private schools but complains about elitism.

Buys wine at the State speciality Wine Store.

Shops Wild Oats, Farmers' Market.

Tries to remember to buy books at Salt Lake's two remaining independent bookstores.

Pronounces "croissant" "croissant."

Takes Eco-Trips.

Plans to move to San Francisco next year.
or Island Park, ID

# The Gay Male Couple

Blond. Thought to be straight because they wear wedding rings.

## Habitat

Loft in Salt Lake's "SOHO" (South of the House of Worship) district purchased 20 years after they became popular and as soon as they arrived in Salt Lake City. Or, live in two bedroom home, with one bedroom that never looks slept in. Home looks professionally decorated and it is not (does not have the "celestial" touches of other Utah homes).

## Characteristics

Drive SUVs.

Have never taken public transportation.

Often mention their "roommate."

Host cookie decorating parties during the holidays.

Plan to move to San Francisco next week.

Will end up in Island Park, ID

# The Lesbian Couple

Blonde. Thought to be straight because they wear wedding rings and are perpetually pregnant.

## Habitat

Commune of battered trailers in the West Desert.

## Characteristics

Not allowed to drive.

Doesn't know public transportation exists.

Wears floral maternity burqa.

Pregnant at 13, married to uncle at 13.1.

Held hostage by husband who basks in the glory of having plural wives in his Kingdom on Earth.

Suffers once-a-month visit from the old goat.

Prefers "companionship" of "sister-wives."

Has never heard of San Francisco.

# The Queen of Zion

Blonde. Kate Spade bag, capris, black slides, lots of makeup.

Uses Prozac® and Retin A®, fake bake (tanning booth) tan, french manicure.

Four blonde kids, drops them off at country club pool.

## Habitat

Found in 5,000 sq. ft. McMansion with "great room" on tiny yard, Pergo floors, master bedroom decorated with "bed in a bag" and 20 decorative pillows. Also found around country club pools.

## Characteristics

Drives SUV.

Has never taken public transportation.

Has gotten husband to go to church "for the kids."

Kids go to public ("Mormon") school in neighborhood or private school if kids from West Side are bused in to public school (thus creating "a mixture," known in other states as "diversity").

Had a career before the kids but can't remember what it was.

Art History Major with a minor in Early Childhood Development, neither of which she intends to use.

Accomplished pianist but not too accomplished so as to concern her in-laws or husband.

Has two business cards (automatically issued upon marriage): one saying she is a caterer the other an interior designer. Has never done either. Will never do either.

Told her husband she was on the pill.

Reads articles about choosing plastic surgeons.

Subscribes to Salt Lake City magazine, looks for friends and enemies in social columns.

Believes Salt Lake City society matters.

Husband gay.

# The West Valley Breeder

### Male

Blond with roots showing.

Backwards baseball cap advertising heavy machinery (John Deere, Peterbuilt, GMC etc.).

Discounted flannel shirt over stained t-shirt with faded pot leaf image or faded 80's rock band logo.

Ass crack showing, with or without tool belt attached.

Needs two seats in restaurants, one for each cheek.

Has dated a first cousin.

### Female

Blonde with roots showing.

Lots of black eyeliner and mascara from the day before.

Dares to wear all of her fashion accessories from Valley Fair Mall. Wears high heels year-round and for every function often with jeans. Has dated at least one first cousin and possible fathered a child by him. Thinks she is still a virgin because she makes him pull out.

### Habitat

Mobile home or twin home (duplex) shared with their 5 kids and the 3 kids of the sister who is in prison and soon with their first grandchild by their teenage daughter.

### Characteristics

Drives a jacked up pickup with really big tires or a SUV modified to accommodate the really big tires. Has never taken public transportation even after third DUI.

First in line at all-you-can-eat-buffet.

Second in line at all-you-can-eat buffet.

Third in line at all-you-can-eat buffet.

Tries to get senior and under five-years-old discounts at all-you-can-eat buffets and movies.

# The Art People

## Male

Blond. Has worn all black since 1980. Suspected of being gay because he doesn't own a motorized recreational vehicle.

## Female

Blonde. Has worn all black since 1980. Resents any younger, prettier or thinner female. Husband allegedly not-gay.

## Habitat

Found in museum-like setting with all white walls and furniture designed to keep the homeless from falling asleep on it. Also found at swank fundraisers attended by all of the same people who can't recall which boards they serve on.

## Characteristics

Drive German cars.

Have never taken public transportation.

Keep social un-equals at bay with haughty glares ("glare 'n' annoy 'em").

Leave Sunday <u>New York Times</u> on porch until mid-afternoon so people will see it.

Think they live in New York.

Require Prozac® to maintain state of self-deception.

# The Counterculture Radical

## Male

Tattoos, piercings, formerly blond, now orange.

## Female

Tattoos, piercings, formerly blonde, now orange.

## Habitat

Coffee houses in university area.

## Characteristics

Drive SUV with bumper sticker condemning petroleum exploration.

Would never take public transportation.

Unaware of world hunger.

Not sure where Pakistan is.

Never been outside of Utah.

Preoccupied with inequality in the social structure of beehives.

Sit in coffee houses.

Smoke cigarettes.

Think about how futile it is to accomplish anything in Utah.

Get tattoos.

Thinks about how messed up it is that their parents made them grow up in Utah.

Think about college.

Think about how institutionalized and oppressive college is.

Get their tongues pierced.

Read Dostoyevsky.

Think about how futile everything is.

Pretend they are in San Francisco.

Think of places they could go.

Don't go.

Drink more coffee.

Call parents for money.

# part nine: The official Utah marriage matrix

## (<u>whom</u> can marry <u>whom</u>)

# Utah Marriage Matrix

The Utah State Legislature meets for only four hours a year now that it gerrymandered the Democratic Party out of existence in 2001, thereby removing all opposition to their Church-sponsored bills. The following Utah Marriage Matrix was passed unanimously in the January 2002 Legislative Session to ease the paperwork at the Mormon Temple.

**Category 1: People who may marry only people in their own category:**

Smith

Young

Cannon

Tanner

Huntsman

Quinney

Romney

Smart

McConkie

Nebeker

Ricks

Kunz

Category 2: People who may marry people in their own category or people in Categories 3 & 4 provided they met on a mission for the LDS church and the person in Category 3 or 4 does not speak with an accent, or wear, for example "La Raza" insignia, or otherwise insist on not giving up their native culture.

Jones

Monroe

Woodruff

Bates

Stein

White

Davis

Bailey

(etc.)

Moulton

Category 3: People who may marry in Category 2-4 (Category 2 subject to conditions set forth above).

Martinez

Jimenez

Ruiz

Alvarez

Flores

Hernandez


**Category 4: People who may marry in Category 2-4 (Category 2 subject to conditions set forth above).**

Chan

Wu

Wong

Lee

Tan


**Category 5: People who may marry in Category 3-4.**

Wansktaiksl

Musieiginsop

Popelsigininh


**Category 6: People who may only marry in their own category.**

Jefferson

Washington

# part ten:

# Utah Drivers' Exam

# Utah Drivers' Exam

Do NOT ask to take this test in a foreign language! English is the official language of the State of Utah and if you cannot speak it you must leave. Now! (And NOT in the driver's seat of a motorized vehicle!) Only our Returned Missionaries are allowed to speak foreign languages and then, only if they are attempting to convert a heathen or attempting to procure unprotected sex potentially leading to marriage with someone within Marriage Categories 3-4.

**In Utah, the concept "the bigger the better" applies to (check all that apply):**

SUVs
snowmobiles
boats
parking lots
parking spaces
roads
food portions
entertainment systems
homes (but not lots)
women
laptop computers

hair
silicone implants
cell phones
**Answer**: All.

**In Utah the concept "the more the better"
applies to (check all that apply):**
freeways
perms
kids
wives
alcohol consumption
handguns
food
Mormon control of the State
Sex education

**Answer**: All but the last.

**If there is no parking space in front of your
destination, you:**
A. Make a mental note to try again
   tomorrow
B. Get out your concealed weapon
C. Double park
D. Use valet parking

**Answer**: A if you are in Salt Lake, B if you
are in Utah County.

## A martini tastes like:

    A. A martini

    B. The female elk urine you can buy in the huntin store to put on yourself to attract male elks

    C. Gasoline

**Answer**: If you said A, you may not drive in Utah; if you said B, you may drive anywhere in Utah; if you said C, please confine yourself to Utah County.

## When you come to a 4-way stop and there are no other cars in sight, you:

    A. Stop, then proceed through the intersection.

    B. Just roll through the intersection.

    C. Stop and wait until another car appears. Then make sure that car stops before proceeding through the intersection.

**Answer**: C. NOTE: It is illegal in Utah to GO at a 4-way stop unless there is another car there to bear witness to it. You MUST WAIT for that other car to appear—even if it takes hours! Then the witness must bear his testimony regarding the legality of the stop in Church the following Sunday.

**Which of the following are true?**
The safest place in a car for a baby is in the mom's lap.

It's better to not wear a seatbelt so you won't get trapped in a burning car.

If Heavenly Father wanted you to wear seatbelts he would have made you with one.

Mormon Doctrine prohibits children who are not yet baptized (under 8) from wearing seatbelts or sitting in car seats.

Motorcycle helmets can obstruct your vision in a dangerous way.

Taking public transportation is un-American.

**Answer**: All of the above.

**True or false?** A Utah legislator objected to seat belt laws on the basis that he wouldn't be able to haul all his kids to Church if they all had to wear seatbelts.

**Answer**: True, As on KUTV News, Nov., 2001.

# Afterward

Please do not take us wrong. We do not hate Mormons. Some of our best friends are Mormons we have met in group therapy or dressed as missionaries seeking same-sex partners on Castro Street in San Francisco. Or at the Poina the Mou'n.

## Outrage others! Buy more copies!

Order additional copies of this book by mail by sending a check made out to Pince-Nez Press to the address below. Enclose $12.95 per book plus sales tax and $2 shipping and handling (book rate) for the first copy and $1 for each additional copy. Or buy with a credit card at **www.pince-nez.com** (click on Order Info). Please, do not drop by our office to deliver any "gifts"–not even Temple Mints. All "gifts" are forwarded to the San Francisco Sheriff's Department Hate Crime Taskforce.

Nez-Perce Press
1459 18th St. PMB 175
San Francisco, CA
(415) 267-5978